Changes in

by Shar

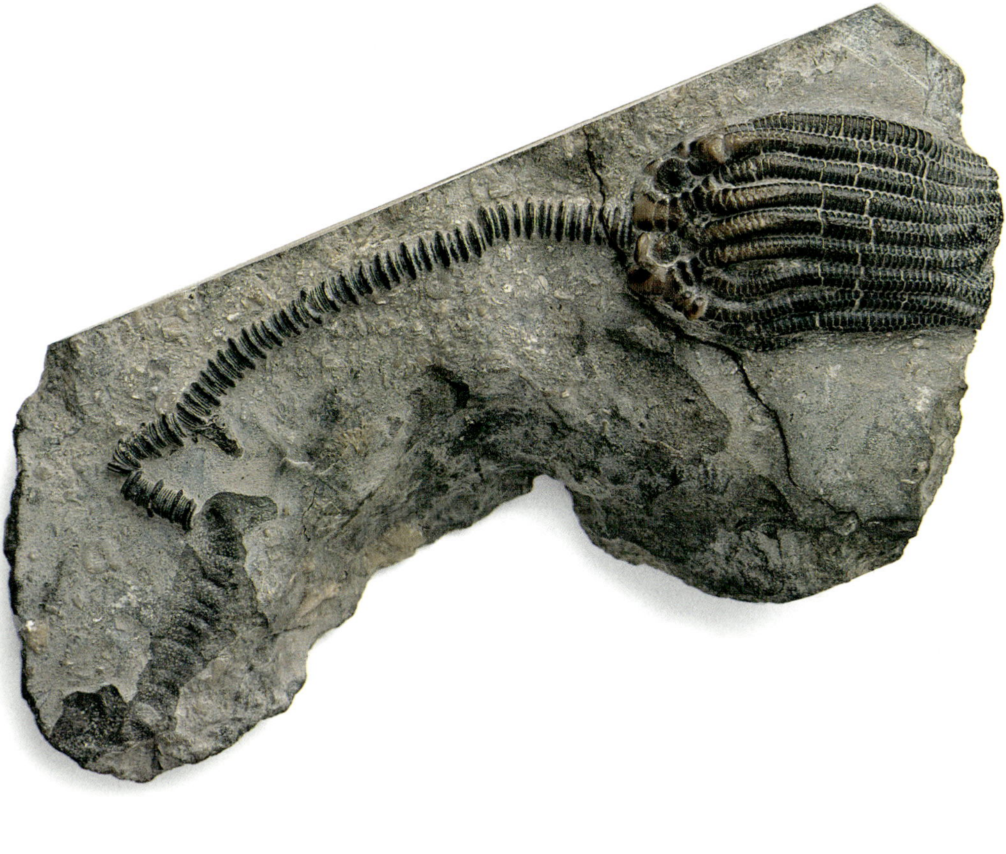

MW01616356

How are ecosystems balanced?

Needs of Living Things

A chipmunk comes out of its forest burrow. It runs up to a mushroom. The mushroom is just one source of food for the chipmunk. This is one of the many ways plants and animals interact in a balanced ecosystem.

The Great Smoky Mountains are home to more than ten thousand kinds of plants and animals. The Eastern American chipmunk is just one.

The chipmunk needs food, air, water, and shelter in order to live. It gets food and air from the forest plants. It gets water from puddles and streams. Forest trees make a safe place to dig a burrow in the ground. The burrow keeps the chipmunk warm. It also keeps the chipmunk safe from predators such as hawks and foxes.

Plants and animals depend on their environment. They need food, air, water, and shelter to be healthy and grow. Good soil and the right weather are also important. Plants and animals can only live in places that meet their needs. The Great Smoky Mountains meet all the Eastern American chipmunk's needs.

The Eastern American chipmunk is one of many species found in the Great Smoky Mountains.

A Balancing Act

An ecosystem is similar to a seesaw. Animals are on one side. Food, space, and shelter are on the other side. In a healthy ecosystem, the seesaw is balanced. If too many animals are added, there will not be enough food or shelter for all of them. The seesaw will not be balanced.

Plants also need a balanced ecosystem. Plants need water, sunlight, the right soil, and enough space. What happens if you plant seeds too close together? Many seeds will not have enough space to grow.

Plants and animals work together to keep an ecosystem in balance. For example, rabbits eat grass. Less grass means more space for other plants to grow. But red foxes eat rabbits. Then there are fewer rabbits to eat the grass. Therefore, more plants grow. The plants produce more air and water that all animals need.

Ecosystems have changes all the time. Living things are born. They live, die, and decompose. The water in ponds can dry up. But rain returns water to the ponds. Animals take in oxygen from the air. Plants put oxygen back into the ecosystem. All these changes help keep ecosystems in balance.

How do organisms interact?

Change in Ecosystems

When an ecosystem's resources change, the number of living things changes. When chipmunks have enough to eat, their population can increase. More chipmunks will use more resources. At some point, there will not be enough food, water, and space for all of the chipmunks. Some will die. Others may move to a new place. With fewer chipmunks, there will again be enough resources. The chipmunk population will increase.

Competing

When different organisms in an ecosystem need the same limited resources, **competition** occurs. Organisms have adaptations that can help them live and grow successfully.

Many organisms compete for living space. Plants compete for light and water. Birds compete for the same places to build nests. Other animals, such as foxes and owls, compete for the same food.

Sharing Resources

Some animals find ways to avoid competing. Hawks and owls both hunt the same animals. But hawks hunt during the day. Owls hunt at night.

Some animals live in groups. Wolves hunt deer together. The deer form tight groups to help keep the herd safe. This makes it harder for a wolf to attack any one deer.

Helping Each Other

Two organisms may live closely together. Sometimes this helps both organisms. Sometimes this helps only one organism. Animals, plants, fungi, protists, and bacteria can have these helpful relationships.

Lichens are fungi and algae that live together. The algae give the fungi nutrients and water. The fungi shelter the algae from the Sun.

Living Side by Side

Oak trees give shelter to moss. The moss neither helps nor harms the oak tree.

Animals can also have this kind of relationship. Silverfish may travel with army ants. The insects eat the food the army ants leave behind. They neither help nor harm the army ants.

Lichens can grow on rocks.

Causing Harm

Sometimes one organism is helped while another is harmed. The organism that is helped is a **parasite.** A parasite lives on or in another organism. The organism that is harmed is the **host.** The host is a source of food for the parasite.

Balsam woolly adelgids are insects that are parasites. They feed on Fraser fir trees. When these parasite insects feed, they harm the trees.

How do environments change?

The Process of Change

What is now a forest area may have been a lake thousands of years ago. But over many years the lake may have dried up. The area became a marsh. Marsh grasses and bushes grew. Then the environment changed more. Trees began to grow. Today the area is a forest. The slow change from one community of organisms to another is **succession.**

Very few living things are in a newly formed lake. Rivers will carry soil into the lake. Algae, bacteria, and spores from fungi may be in the soil.

These organisms add nutrients to the lake. Now small plants can grow. Herbivores will move into the ecosystem.

One Step at a Time

Succession usually takes place in stages. For example, bare land might first change to grassland. Next, shrubs may begin to grow. Then, over time, the shrub land may become forest. Areas continue to grow and change until there is a balance. For a time there are few changes.

Average temperature, winds, and rainfall over many years make up an area's climate. Changes in climate slowly affect ecosystems. Parts of North America were covered in snow and ice more than fifteen thousand years ago. No trees, grasses, or flowering plants could grow in the cold climate. But slowly the climate grew warmer. Then plants could grow, and animals could live there. Over time the forests we see today were formed.

Many animals and plants now live and interact in this community. Slowly the lake fills with soil, leaves, and decomposing organisms. The lake becomes a marsh.

Eventually the marsh fills and dries up. Trees begin to grow. The marsh is changing into a forest.

Changing Species

In the 1800s and early 1900s, many passenger pigeons flew over the Great Smoky Mountains. But by 1915 not one passenger pigeon was left. The species had become **extinct,** or died out. Why do living things become extinct?

Sometimes species will not survive if the environment changes. In the past, volcanoes, climate changes, and meteors caused animals to become extinct. Today, most animals become extinct for two reasons. Their homes are destroyed, and they have no place to live. Other animals are hunted until they are extinct. A species usually cannot survive once its number drops below a certain level.

Passenger pigeon

Some species have such small populations that they are in danger of becoming extinct. They are called **endangered** species. Species that may soon be endangered are called threatened species. Endangered and threatened species may leave their environments. They may try to find another place to live.

Some species are saved from becoming extinct. In 1970 the peregrine falcon was endangered. Many people worked together to help save this species. By 1999, its population had grown so that it was no longer endangered.

Peregrine falcon

Species Then and Now

How do we know how species have changed over time? To find out, scientists study fossils. They compare fossils from long ago with organisms that are alive today.

Woolly mammoths became extinct long ago. Some were frozen solid in ice. Scientists have learned about them from their fossils. Scientists compare them with elephants of today. Both animals have large tusks and long noses. Their skeletons are very similar. The woolly mammoth and modern-day elephants are so alike that scientists group them in the same family.

Many sea lilies have been preserved as fossils.

Fossils can tell us about life on Earth long ago. Fossils help us understand past environmental changes. Scientists may find marine animal fossils in dry climates. This tells scientists that a big change happened. It tells them that shallow seas once covered what is now a dry area.

Few species of sea lilies remain. They attach themselves to the ocean floor.

Rapid Changes

A hurricane's strong winds rip up trees. Heavy rains and giant waves flood coastal towns. One lightning strike can set an entire forest on fire.

Other natural events, such as earthquakes and volcanic eruptions, can also change an environment in an instant. These changes can mean that some species must find a new home because the resources they need are gone.

Sometimes natural events can help keep the environment in balance. Forest fires burn dead and dying plants, making room for new plants to grow. The Table Mountain pine tree has cones that open in the heat of a fire. Then new pine trees can grow.

Fires spread quickly when they come across dead branches, dried leaves, and rotting plants.

Natural Disasters

In 1993, very heavy rain caused the Mississippi and Missouri Rivers to overflow. Some areas of land were flooded for almost seven months. The waters left large areas of land covered with sand and mud.

The flooding killed many trees and grasses. Birds lost nesting places and had fewer babies. However, some fish populations increased. The water gave the fish new areas in which to feed and reproduce.

Fires can destroy entire forests. But they also can help new plants to grow.

How do people disturb the balance?

People and the Environment

Like other organisms, we depend on our environment for food, water, and shelter. But unlike other organisms, we can change our environment in various ways to meet our needs. We cut down trees for lumber. We clear land to plant crops. We build roads through forests. Each change can upset the balance of the ecosystem.

Sometimes we put wastes into the environment that upset the ecosystem. Harmful gases, dust, dirt, and other wastes pollute the air and water. Cars and factories put harmful chemicals into the air. These chemicals can harm people. They can damage plants. They may cause animals to lose food or shelter.

Polluted Water

Wastes and chemicals can also pollute rivers, lakes, and oceans. Some wastes are dumped right into the water through sewer systems. Chemicals are used on land to grow plants or kill insects. Rain washes the chemicals into lakes and rivers. The chemicals can kill the plants and animals that live there.

Chemicals and other kinds of pollution in rivers and streams can flow into the oceans. Oil spills and leaks sometimes happen during the drilling and shipping of oil. This pollutes the ocean. Ocean plants, fish, and birds are coated with oil. The birds often drown.

The Cuyahoga River was heavily polluted with oil, logs, and other wastes. In 1952 it caught fire. This led to the Clean Water Act, which makes it illegal to pollute water.

Land Pollution

Did you know that every person throws away about two kilograms, or almost four and a half pounds, of garbage every day? Most trash is dumped in landfills. Then it is covered with soil. Garbage, litter, and other materials can cause pollution.

Another kind of land pollution is caused by **hazardous waste.** Hazardous waste harms humans and other organisms. Some hazardous waste is poison. It can cause diseases. Other waste can start fires. It can react in dangerous ways with other materials. Until recently, most hazardous waste was put into containers that were buried in the ground. Some containers leaked. The waste went into the ground and damaged the environment.

Stripping Away the Land

Many valuable substances are under the surface of Earth. Coal is one example. Strip mining is a way to get coal out of the ground. Big machines dig up and clear away the top layers of soil. The digging leaves huge pits. No trees, rocks, or plants are left to hold the dirt. Over time the land begins to erode. The dirt and rocks wash into nearby rivers and ponds. Ecosystems surrounding these areas are greatly affected.

It is important to restore the land so animals can return or so the land can be used to grow crops.

Land Reclamation

Federal laws now make mining companies replace the rock and soil they remove. They must replant the area with native trees and grasses. This is known as reclaiming.

Coal mining began in some states in the 1840s. Damage to the land was not fixed for more than 100 years. In the 1970s new laws were passed. They changed how mining could be done. One law requires coal companies to study an ecosystem before mining. They must have a plan on how they will reclaim the land.

California has reclaimed several mining areas. A gravel pit in Sacramento County is once again a water environment. Other mined areas now grow alfalfa, corn, and strawberries.

Preserving the Environment

Our nation is full of beautiful natural areas. Visitors look down into the Grand Canyon's vast depths. Others watch millions of gallons of water rush over Niagara Falls.

One way to keep special places safe is to develop national parks. People can visit national parks and enjoy these beautiful areas.

Organisms interact within an ecosystem. Some relationships help both organisms, while some relationships help only one organism. Some relationships may even harm one organism. Environmental changes can happen quickly or slowly. People can cause a great deal of change within an environment. It is important that we help keep the balance of all ecosystems.

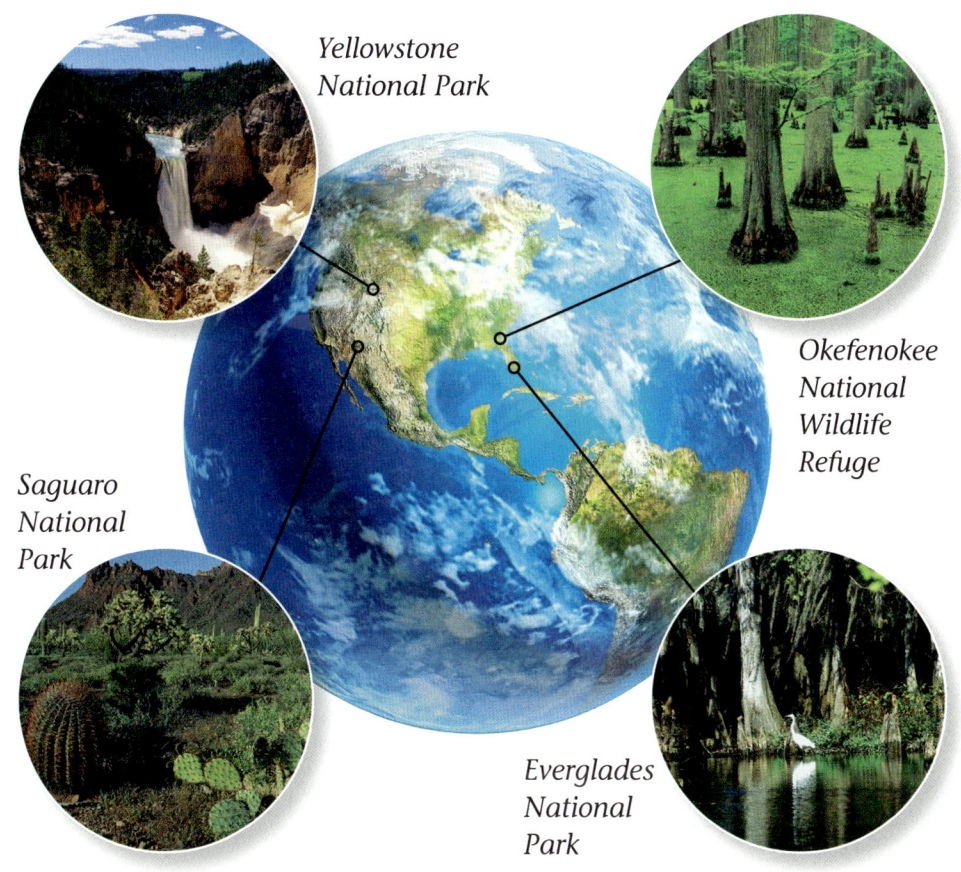

Yellowstone National Park

Okefenokee National Wildlife Refuge

Saguaro National Park

Everglades National Park

Glossary

competition   the struggle among organisms to get what they need to live and reproduce

endangered   in danger of becoming extinct because so few members of the species are left

extinct   no longer existing; usually referring to a species

hazardous waste   materials that are harmful to people, to other organisms, and to the environment

host   an organism that provides food or shelter to another living thing

parasite   an organism that harms the host it lives on or in

succession   a slow change over time from one community of organisms to another